D1456736

Mrs. Beaver and the Wolf at the Door

Written by Christopher A. Lane
Illustrated by Sharon Dahl

A SonFlower Book

VICTOR BOOKS®

A DIVISION OF SCRIPTURE PRESS PUBLICATIONS INC.
USA CANADA ENGLAND

Dedicated
to Grandmother, the lookout:
"They're here!"
And in loving memory of Pappy,
the napper: "What, what?!"

KIDDERMINSTER KINGDOM TALES
King Leonard's Celebration
Sir Humphrey's Honeystands
Nicholas and His Neighbors
Cornelius T. Mouse and Sons
King Leonard's Great Grape Harvest
Mrs. Beaver and the Wolf at the Door

1 2 3 4 5 6 7 8 9 10 Printing/Year 94 93 92 91

ISBN: 0-89693-269-9

© 1991 SP Publications, Inc. All rights reserved.

VICTOR BOOKS
A division of SP Publications, Inc.
Wheaton, Illinois 60187

Mrs. Beaver and the Wolf at the Door

I n the Kingdom of Kidderminster there was once a beaver named Barney who lived with his wife Beatrice on a golden pond at the edge of the forest. Their beautiful home was made out of fine logs which Barney had selected himself, diligently chewed to fit, and carefully set into place in the center of a babbling brook. Beatrice had taken charge of the inside of their house, pasting up flowered wallpaper in the kitchen and bath, and painting the other rooms pleasant shades. She hung curtains over the small living room window, and helped Barney build their furniture. It took them some time, but together Mr. and Mrs. Beaver had built a warm, cozy dam in which to live.

It came about one day, when they had grown old and gray, that tragedy struck. Barney fell off the roof. A doctor was summoned, and did his best, but Barney didn't make it through the night.

The next day, animals from across the kingdom gathered at the Beaver home. All of the forest creatures were there, as were Cornelius T. Mouse and his two sons, and Nicholas the cat and his friend Ned the dog. King Leonard, though unable to attend himself, sent Horatio, his servant, with a letter of sympathy and encouragement to Mrs. Beaver. Sir Humphrey, the wealthy business bear, addressed the crowd with a few words about Mr. Beaver, who had once worked for him as a furniture maker.

"Those who knew Barney," the bear growled, "loved Barney. A kinder, more faithful animal you couldn't hope to meet. Any time there was wood to be whittled, chewed, or fitted, Barney Beaver was the one to call. He was an inspiration to woodworkers and beavers everywhere. We will all miss him dearly.

"And now," Sir Humphrey said in a gentle tone, "I speak for all of the good animals here as I extend our deepest regrets to his widow, Beatrice."

It was quite a ceremony. Though Mr. Beaver had not been rich or famous, he had been fair and just and was well liked by all.

When her friends and family had returned to their own homes, Beatrice sat inside her house and cried for a whole week straight. She was so sad and lonely that she cried until she felt she could cry no longer, and then she cried some more.

One day, after her sniffles had finally passed, Beatrice was in the kitchen. It had been her habit for some years to make special treats to surprise her neighbors with, and on this particular day she was making a basket of maple nut scones and a kettle of sawdust tea for the porcupine family across the brook. Just as she was preparing to wrap up the goodies, there came a knock at the door. After checking her face and fur in the hall mirror, she opened the door and discovered two animals standing outside talking.

"It's the perfect place, Sir," a skinny weasel was saying.

"I suppose," a large gray wolf wearing a fine coat and top hat said. "What about this brook?"

"No problem," the weasel said, gesturing with his paws. "After we get rid of this old house, we'll stop up this brook and build right here. Your hotel will fit neatly here next to the pond. I can see it now — " 'The Wolf's Den Hotel.' "

"Ahem." Beatrice cleared her throat to gain their attention. "Is there something I can help you with?"

"Ah, Madame," the weasel said with a smile, "good day."

"Good day to you, Sir," she answered warily. "And what might be your business here?"

"This will explain everything," he said, handing her a sheet of paper.

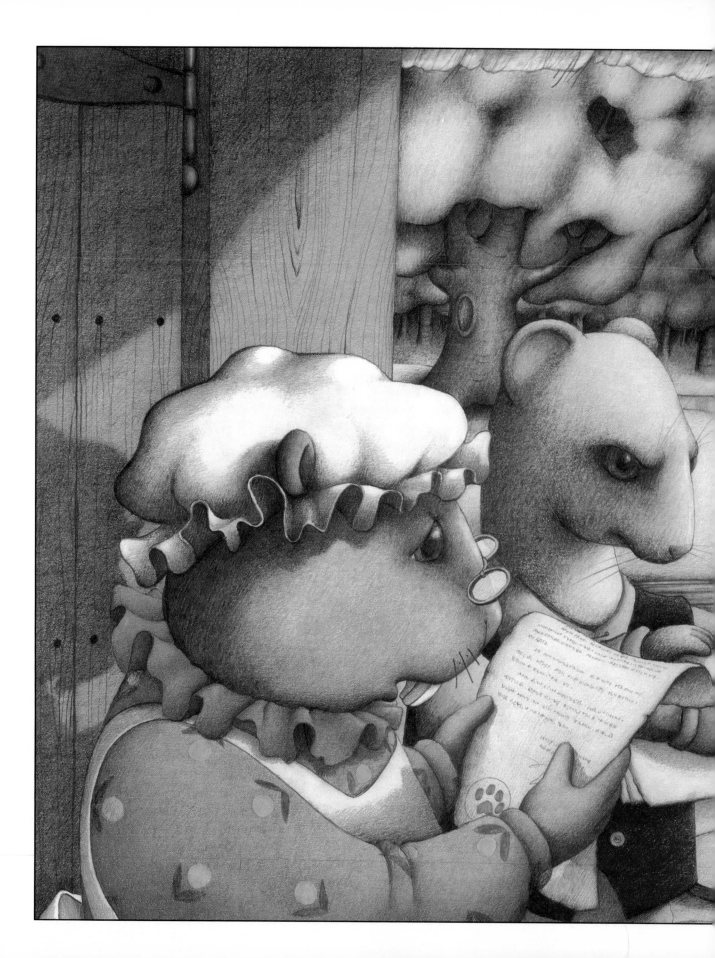

The note said: *"Your home is now the property of the J.B. Wolf Company. You and all of your possessions must be off the premises by tomorrow, or else!"*

"What!" Beatrice was shocked. "Why, you can't do this. This is my home!"

"Correction, lady," the weasel said, rather impatiently. "It *was* your home." He shuffled through a file of papers in his hand. "Says right here, that after Mr. Barney Beaver died last week, the title deed was transferred to our company. Unless you have the resources to buy it back, it's time for you to hit the road."

"But, but . . . ! I insist on speaking with your superior!" Beatrice demanded.

"Very well," the weasel said proudly, pointing to his companion. "Let me introduce Mr. J.B. Wolf, robber baron extrordinaire."

The wolf smiled, revealing a mouth full of sharp teeth. "Good day, Mrs. Beaver. Your house is now my property and you and your things must be out by tomorrow."

"We'll just see about that," Beatrice fumed.

"We certainly will. Good day, Madame," the wolf said, tipping his hat as the beaver closed the door.

"Good work, Sir," the weasel giggled. "You sure scared her."

Though she had tried to sound brave, Beatrice was quite worried. Who were these strangers? Could they really take away her home?

"Sir Humphrey," she suddenly thought. "He is the most respected animal in all the forest. If anyone can help me, it is that wealthy bear."

After collecting her purse, her hat, and scarf, Beatrice scurried off through the forest to Sir Humphrey's mansion. But when she arrived, she was disappointed to find that he was not at home. As his butler, Reginald, told it, King Leonard had requested that Sir Humphrey open one of his honeystands in the jungle so the jungle animals could be supplied with honey. The bear had left to attend to it personally.

Beatrice was about to lose all hope when Reginald suggested that she see Judge Kensington. He explained that the judge was a wise elk who represented King Leonard in the forest and who judged various arguments between woodland creatures. Judge Kensington was an expert in the law, and according to Reginald, he would be able to keep the wolf from taking the widow's home. The butler warned, however, that the judge was an ornery old elk who enjoyed his privacy and wasn't overly fond of animals.

Beatrice wasn't sure just what that meant, but she knew she had to see the judge. So after Reginald hailed her a carriage, she set out for the courthouse, a lengthy trip that took her across the whole of the forest. When she finally arrived, it was past lunchtime, and since her breakfast had been rudely interrupted, she was quite hungry. Her empty stomach urged her to stop for a bowl of soup or a hot cross bun, but she decided against it. This needed to be settled right away.

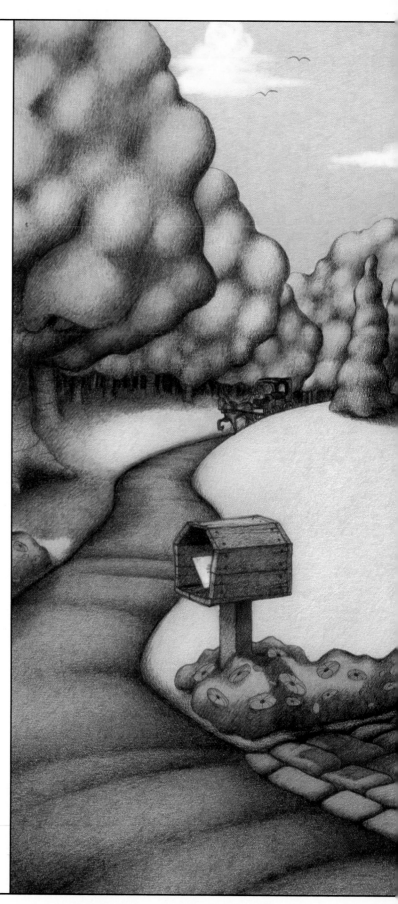

"My name is Mrs. Beatrice Beaver and I have a request to make of Judge Kensington," she told the young crow sitting at a desk in the entryway of the courthouse.

"Do you have an appointment?" the bird cawed sleepily, never looking up from her work.

"No, but it is a matter of some urgency," Beatrice explained.

"The judge is a busy elk," the crow said with a cock of her head. "He does not have time to see just anyone and everyone who walks in the door."

"But my home is about to be taken from me," Beatrice said.

"I don't care if the forest is on fire," the crow snipped. "If you don't have an appointment, you can't see the judge."

"When can I get an appointment?" Beatrice asked.

The crow leafed lazily through a calendar on her desk. "How's two weeks from next Thursday sound?"

"That's much too late," Beatrice objected. "I simply must see him today! It's an emergency!"

The crow was ignoring her now, busy primping her feathers.

Beatrice could have given up right then and there, and no one would have blamed her if she had. But as she stood looking at the sassy young crow who didn't seem to care at all about her predicament, she made a decision. She decided that no matter what, she was going to see the judge and keep her home.

When Beatrice walked out the front door of the courthouse, the crow thought she had seen the last of her. Little did she know that the enterprising old beaver simply went around back and slipped through a service entrance used by the maids and cooks.

Inside Beatrice found a long hallway which was perfectly quiet, except for the occasional clanging of a kettle or pan as the cooks prepared refreshments for teatime. She had no idea which room the judge might be in, so she began walking down the hall, pausing to listen outside each and every doorway. Eventually she came to a large oak door. It had a shiny brass knob and a slate-green plaque which read: *"Behind these doors sits a fair judge committed to what is right and just."*

"This must be the one," she said to herself.

She tapped on the door, lightly at first, and then when no one answered, she gave it a sharp rap. Nothing happened. She considered trying the knob, but then decided against it. It was one thing to bypass the rude secretary in her attempt to see the judge. It was quite another to barge into his office.

Then she spotted a window above the door.

"If only I had a ladder," she thought, looking down the hall. All she saw was a serving cart filled with dirty dishes which had not yet been returned to the kitchen. "Hmm . . ." she said thoughtfully.

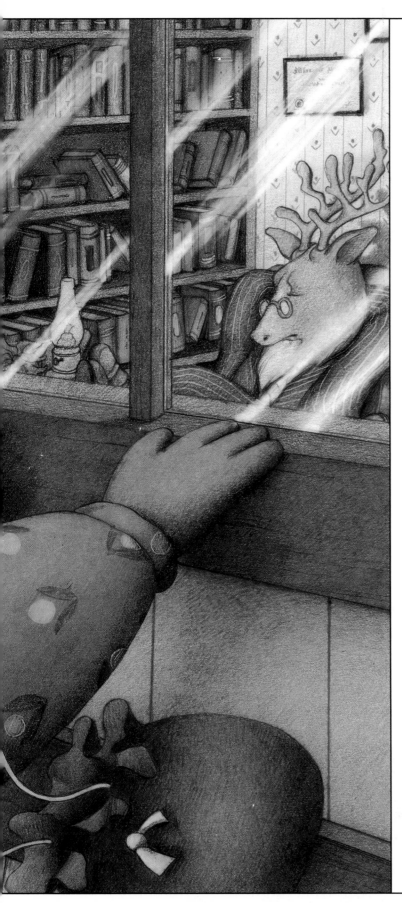

Taking the dishes from the cart, she stacked them neatly on the floor and wheeled it in front of the door. Climbing up onto it, the elderly beaver steadied herself with her tail and strained to look through the high window. What she saw was a room filled with books. There were shelves and shelves of tall, thick, impressive-looking volumes reaching up to the ceiling. In the center of the room was a large wooden desk, behind which sat a chubby, gray-haired elk dressed in a ruffled brown suit and wearing a pair of round spectacles beneath a broad rack of antlers. Squinting to get a better look, Beatrice noticed that his eyes were closed. The judge was dozing!

Suddenly the cart began to roll and Beatrice lost her balance. Gripping the edge of the window sill, she hung on with all her might.

"Help!" she screamed. "Help me!"

This startled the judge, who jumped out of his chair and came running out of his office at a gallop — only to have Beatrice fall into his arms as he passed through the door.

"What? Who are you?" the surprised elk asked as he put her down. "And what are you doing hanging around outside my office?"

By this time the crow from the entryway had arrived on the scene along with a collection of the servants and cooks. Beatrice was embarrassed by the crowd and nearly turned tail to run until she remembered why she had come.

"My name is Mrs. Beatrice Beaver and I have an urgent request, Sir," she finally blurted out.

"What is this all about, Miss Birdie?" the judge asked the crow. "Why have you allowed this beaver to bother me?"

"I apologize, Sir," the crow squawked. "I told her you were busy. Come along, you."

"But I must talk with you, Sir," Beatrice pleaded as the servants carried her off down the hallway. "It is about my home . . ."

"Make an appointment like everyone else," the judge grumbled. "Now, where was I?" he asked himself as he returned to his office, slamming the door.

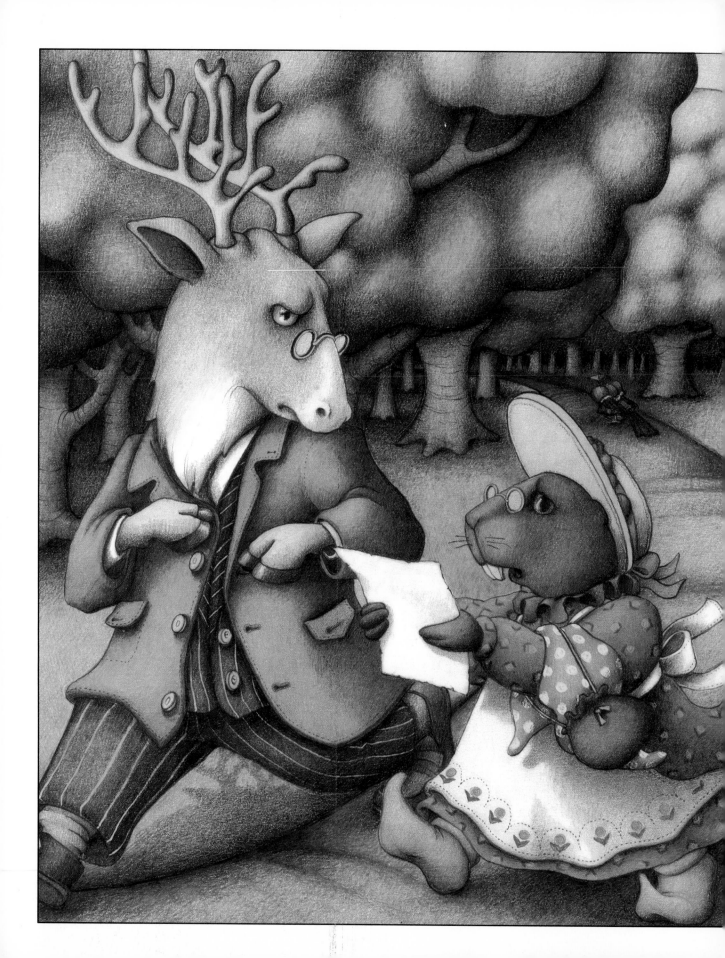

Sitting on the steps outside the courthouse, Beatrice wondered what she should do. As the hours passed and the sun slipped down toward the horizon, she thought as hard as she could think, but no plan came to mind. It seemed that she would lose her home for certain.

Then she heard a door close behind her and turned around to see the judge and the crow leaving the courthouse.

"Good-night, Miss Birdie," Judge Kensington said, pulling on his long coat.

"Good-night, Sir," the crow replied.

After the crow had hopped out of sight, Beatrice caught up to the judge. "Judge Kensington, I must see you!"

"Oh, not you again." The pudgy elk shook his head.

"It's urgent! I must talk to you today!"

"I'm going home," he snorted. "I suggest you do the same." And he walked away at a brisk pace.

Beatrice had to run just to keep the important elk in sight. Every so often he would stop and look over his shoulder at her, and then continue on all the faster.

When the judge reached his home, he hurriedly unlocked the door and rushed in, leaving Beatrice standing in the street. Inside he gave a sigh of relief, thinking that now the pesky beaver would surely become discouraged and leave him alone. But he was mistaken.

First there was a knock on the door. The judge knew it was Beatrice and decided not to answer it. Then there came a tapping at the window, but the judge kept the curtains drawn. Next a rock with a note attached to it came bouncing down the chimney, but he refused to read it. All was quiet for several minutes and the ornery elk began to think that the beaver had finally given up and left. As he quietly chuckled to himself at having outlasted her, he heard a strange noise outside.

"Judge Kensington!" Beatrice hollered at the top of her voice. "Please hear my request! Won't you come to the aid of an old widow? Won't you defend an elderly beaver? Please, oh, please, won't you help me keep my home? Don't you care about what's just and fair? Aren't you a servant of the lion, King Leonard?"

Beatrice was making such a racket that the judge feared his neighbors would hear and begin asking questions. The old beaver was becoming an embarrassment. He threw open the door.

"Stop it!" the judge pleaded. "I'll do anything you ask!"

"Then you are just and fair?" Beatrice was surprised.

"I am nothing of the sort," the judge said angrily.

"Well, you are at the very least a servant of King Leonard."

"I have not the slightest respect for him, either," the elk scoffed.

"Then why have you decided to help me?" Beatrice asked, more puzzled than ever.

"Because you persist in bothering me," he grumbled. "I will see to it that your request is granted, Mrs. Beaver, if you will simply promise to leave me alone."

Beatrice nodded her head in agreement.

"Now, what is your request?" he asked.

Beatrice began to explain her problem to the grumpy elk, telling him about her late husband and the notice she had been given by the nasty weasel and the wicked wolf. When she had finished, he examined the notice carefully.

"No, no, no," he said with a wave of his hoof. "This is all wrong. They have no right to take your home away."

"They don't?" Mrs. Beaver gasped.

"Here," the elk said gruffly, scribbling a message on the bottom of the notice. "This will take care of the problem. Now I insist that you leave me alone, once and for all!" And he trotted back inside his house and slammed the door.

"Thank you, Judge Kensington," Beatrice shouted through the closed door. "I appreciate this favor, no matter what the reason behind it."

After spending the better part of the night traveling, Beatrice finally reached her home just as the sun was coming up. The events of the past day had left her weary and as she prepared for bed, she felt as if she could sleep for a week. But just as she was pulling the warm covers up around her neck, she heard a knock at the door. Tired as she was, she hopped up, put on her robe, and after checking her face and fur in the hall mirror, opened the door.

It was the weasel and the wolf. "Can't you read, lady?" the weasel said fiercely, pushing his way inside. "You've got an hour to gather your things and get out! You see those guys over there?" he asked, pointing to a group of large, scruffy animals standing by with a collection of saws and hammers. "When Mr. Wolf gives the signal, they're gonna tear this place down."

"Well, perhaps Mr. Wolf should see this," Beatrice said with a smile, handing him the notice.

The weasel's jaw dropped as he read it: *"This notice is judged to be illegal. The J.B. Wolf Company has no right to claim the home of Beatrice Beaver. By order of Judge Kensington, you are hereby required to leave her alone."*

With his tail drooping down between his legs, the weasel turned to give the news to his boss. Bowing and cringing, he babbled a series of feeble excuses, and finally handed the notice to Mr. Wolf.

The wolf read it quickly and then slowly bared his fangs. After giving the weasel a long angry look, he started to growl.

"I should have known not to trust a weasel with a wolf's job," the wolf said. "You have upset me for the last time!"

Just as the wolf lunged, the weasel bolted for the road. The wolf took up chase, snapping at his heels as they ran in circles down the road. Beatrice couldn't quite make out what the wolf was saying, but she knew for certain they were not kind words.

"Won't you stay for breakfast?" she called after them, as a peaceful smile spread across her wrinkled face. But they were already too far away to hear.

The sight of the wolf chasing the weasel down the road and the assurance that her house was no longer in danger made Beatrice so happy that she decided not to go back to bed. Instead, the old widow skipped back inside her beautiful log home with a step as spry as that of a young beaver and set about fixing baskets of maple nut scones for her neighbors down the way.

The End

You can read a story like this in the Bible. Jesus told it in Luke 18:1-7:

Then Jesus told His disciples a parable to show them that they should always pray and not give up. He said: "In a certain town there was a judge who neither feared God nor cared about men. And there was a widow in that town who kept coming to him with the plea, 'Grant me justice against my adversary.'

"For some time he refused. But finally he said to himself, 'Even though I don't fear God or care about men, yet because this widow keeps bothering me, I will see that she gets justice, so that she won't eventually wear me out with her coming!' "

And the Lord said, "Listen to what the unjust judge says. And will not God bring about justice for His chosen ones, who cry out to Him day and night? Will He keep putting them off? I tell you, He will see that they get justice, and quickly."